YAKALOU MEDIA

50 Questions to Ask Yourself Before Divorcing Your Partner

You Don't Have To Wonder, "what If?" Or Stay Stuck In Fear

Contents

Disclaimer

This book is designed to provide information only. This information is provided and sold with the knowledge that the publisher and author do not offer any legal or other professional advice. In the case of a need for any such expertise, consult with the appropriate professional.

This book does not contain all the information available on the subject. This book has not been created to be specific to any individual's or organization's situation or needs. Every effort has been made to make this book as accurate as possible. However, there may be typographical and/or content errors. Therefore, this book should serve only as a general guide, not as the ultimate source of subject information.

This book contains information that might be dated and is intended only to educate and entertain. Regarding any loss or damage allegedly suffered or alleged to have occurred as a result of the information in this book, either directly or indirectly, the author and publisher shall have no liability or responsibility to any person or entity.

I

Let's Start Here

Introduction: Let's Talk About the Big Question

If you're holding this book, you're likely standing at one of the toughest crossroads in life, wondering if it's time to walk away or if there's a way to make things work. Maybe you're tired of the constant arguments, the feelings of being misunderstood, or the silent distance that's crept between you and your partner. Or maybe it's just a nagging feeling that something isn't quite right. And here's the thing: wondering "Should I stay, or should I go?" is a big, brave question. It takes courage to even consider it because the answer, whatever it may be, will change your life.

So, why read a book on it? Well, relationships are tricky, complex things. They don't come with a guidebook, and most of us are figuring it out as we go, doing our best to balance love, respect, and our own needs. And when things start to fall apart, it's easy to get lost in the sea of emotions and questions. You might find yourself swinging between reasons to stay and reasons to leave, and that emotional ping-pong match can feel exhausting. This book is here to help you press pause, step back, and ask the questions that matter—so you don't end up stuck in a cycle of confusion, regret, or "what ifs."

Maybe you've even turned to friends or family for advice. And while they mean well, let's be honest—they're often biased, overly optimistic, or ready to hand you a one-size-fits-all solution. But every relationship is unique, and you deserve more than vague advice or "just follow your heart" clichés. This book is different. It doesn't tell you what to do; it guides you to figure out what *you* truly want, with a roadmap of questions designed to get to the core of what's happening in your relationship.

Each chapter is crafted to dive into a different aspect of your relationship, asking questions that cut through the surface stuff and get right to the heart of what's bothering you. We'll explore everything from those normal ups and downs to the possible deal-breakers. Some questions might feel uncomfortable, some might even be a bit humorous (because let's face it, relationships are funny in their own way), but they're all here to help you find clarity and peace.

And clarity—that's the golden ticket here. This isn't about choosing what's easy; it's about choosing what's right for you. Because whether you decide to stay and work things out or take the step toward something new, you deserve to make that choice with confidence, knowing you've examined every angle. No regrets, no lingering "what ifs," just a well-thought-out decision that you can truly stand by.

So let's jump in. Let's untangle the questions, face the fears, and find out what your heart—and your mind—really want. With a little patience, some open reflection, and a willingness to ask yourself the real questions, this journey can lead you to the clarity you've been searching for.

The 7 Rules to Get the Most Out of This Book

Welcome! You've taken the first step by picking up this book, and that's no small feat. But to get the most out of it, a bit of prep work and intention-setting can go a long way. Think of these seven rules as your personal guide to digging deep, staying open, and finding the clarity you deserve. Ready to dive in? Here's how to make this book really work for you.

Rule #1: Be Honest with Yourself

Let's start with the big one: honesty. We're not talking about "Did I eat the last cookie?" kind of honesty, but the kind where you're completely open with yourself about what you feel, want, and need. This book is designed to help you peel back the layers, and that only works if you're willing to be real. Is something bothering you? Do certain questions stir up emotions you'd rather ignore? That's a good sign you're touching on something important. Honesty here will unlock insights that no one else's advice could give you.

Rule #2: Take Your Time

Some of the questions in this book might feel like they need an instant answer, but resist that urge! Good things take time, and so does getting clear on your feelings. This isn't a race, so give yourself permission to read slowly, think carefully, and come back to questions as often as needed. Don't worry if an answer doesn't come immediately. Sometimes, the best insights emerge when we're patient, letting the thoughts simmer until they reveal something meaningful.

Rule #3: Write Down Your Answers

Yes, actually write them down. There's something about putting thoughts on paper (or in a notes app, if you prefer) that makes them feel more concrete. Writing helps you capture those fleeting thoughts and gives you something tangible to come back to, especially if you're feeling confused. It's like having a conversation with yourself that you can revisit later on. So grab a notebook or open a new doc—whatever works for you—and start jotting down your reflections as you go.

Rule #4: Stay Curious

Approach each question with a sense of curiosity, as if you're getting to know yourself all over again. It's easy to think we already know all there is to know about ourselves, but sometimes, the most surprising insights come when we open our minds to new possibilities. Is there an answer you didn't expect? Are there patterns you didn't see before? Embrace these discoveries with curiosity, rather than judgment. This book is about exploring, not judging, so give yourself the freedom to wonder and be surprised.

Rule #5: Expect Some Uncomfortable Moments

Let's be real: not every question will be easy to answer. Some may bring up painful memories or tricky feelings, and that's okay. In fact, that's part of the process. Real clarity often comes from facing those uncomfortable truths head-on. So if you feel a little uneasy or even defensive while reading a question, pause and give yourself a moment to sit with it. Often, the hardest questions bring the most powerful answers. Remember, discomfort isn't a bad thing—it's often where growth begins.

Rule #6: Don't Seek "Right" or "Wrong" Answers

This book isn't a test, and there's no "right" or "wrong" answer here. Every relationship, every situation, and every person is different, so your answers are unique to you. Avoid the temptation to find "correct" responses and instead focus on what feels true to you. The goal here is not to be perfect but to be authentic. Let your responses be messy, raw, and honest. The more real you are with yourself, the clearer your path will become.

Rule #7: Keep Your Eye on Clarity, Not Perfection

Remember, the ultimate goal here isn't to get everything perfect. It's to find clarity—clarity about your feelings, your relationship, and what's next for you. Life doesn't come with a perfect roadmap, and neither does this book. If you feel more grounded, more certain, and more at peace with your decision by the end, then you've done exactly what you set out to do. Focus on finding what feels right, not perfect, and let that be enough.

So there you have it—the seven rules to get the most out of this book. Take these tips to heart, let them guide you, and trust the process. This journey is yours, and with a little honesty, patience, and courage, you'll find the clarity you've been searching for. Let's get started.

Word of Warning Before We Start

Before we jump into the heart of this book, let's pause for a moment. This journey you're about to take is an honest, sometimes intense dive into your relationship, your emotions, and your future. And while that's powerful, it's also something to approach with care. This chapter isn't here to scare you off, but to offer a word of warning—to remind you that this process isn't easy, and to help you prepare for what's ahead. Are you ready to get started?

First things first: the questions in this book might bring up feelings you didn't expect. You might feel hopeful one minute, discouraged the next. That's all part of the journey. It's natural to experience ups and downs when you're reflecting deeply on something as personal as your relationship. So, don't be alarmed if your emotions feel a bit all over the place. Instead, recognize those feelings as part of the process and allow yourself to sit with them. Ask yourself: *Am I willing to face whatever emotions may come up, knowing they're a necessary part of finding clarity?*

Here's another thing to keep in mind: some questions might challenge the way you see yourself and your relationship. You may discover things about yourself that feel uncomfortable, or notice patterns you hadn't seen before. These realizations can be eye-opening, but they can also be a little unsettling. And that's okay. Personal growth and self-discovery rarely come without a little discomfort. Think of it like a spring cleaning for your mind and heart. Sometimes, you have to make a bit of a mess to find what truly matters underneath. So, ask yourself: *Am I prepared to dig deeper, even if it reveals things I didn't expect?*

It's also important to remember that this book won't hand you easy answers. You won't find any one-size-fits-all solutions here. The truth is, only you know what's right for you. This book is a guide—a tool to help you get in touch with your own truth. You might be tempted to look for "the answer" in these pages, but clarity will come from within. So, as you go through each question, let go of any urge to find the "right" answer and instead focus on finding *your* answer. Ask yourself: *Am I willing to embrace uncertainty and trust that the answers will come when I'm ready?*

And here's a gentle reminder: this process takes time. Reflection isn't something you can rush. Each question deserves your patience and honesty, and some answers may take longer to unfold. You may even find that your responses change over time as you dig deeper. That's all part of it. Give yourself the time and grace to work through each chapter at your own pace, without pressuring yourself to reach a conclusion before you're ready. So, ask yourself: *Can I give myself the patience and time I need to find my way through this?*

Lastly, remember that whatever you uncover, you're not alone. Many people have stood exactly where you are—at the crossroads, looking for clarity, feeling a mix of hope and hesitation. Lean on the people who support you, whether that's a friend, a family member, or a counselor. Sometimes, sharing your journey can bring a sense of relief and help you process what you're learning. Don't hesitate to reach out if you need a listening ear or a bit of guidance along the way. Ask yourself: *Am I willing to seek support if the journey feels heavy?*

So, here's the word of warning: this won't be easy, but it will be worth it. By taking this journey seriously, by being brave enough to face your feelings and honest enough to answer each question thoughtfully, you're giving yourself the greatest gift: clarity. Clarity about what you need, what you deserve, and what path is right for you.

Now that you're ready and aware of what lies ahead, take a deep breath, and know that you're capable of whatever this journey reveals. Let's start this journey together, one question at a time.

Read What You Need

Good news: you don't have to read this whole book. Yep, you heard that right! This isn't a novel, a textbook, or a strict journey from cover to cover. Think of it more like a toolkit— one you can dip into anytime you're looking for insight, clarity, or even a little nudge in the right direction. The questions in here are designed to help you navigate your relationship, so it's completely okay to skip around, follow your curiosity, and land where you need to be in the moment.

Maybe you're dealing with a very specific issue right now— like communication struggles or lingering doubts about the future. In that case, go ahead and head straight to those sections. Or perhaps you're feeling stuck in a swirl of emotions without knowing exactly what's wrong. Skim through a few questions and see which ones resonate or bring up a response. Trust your instincts and follow what feels relevant because this book is here to help you.

And some days, you might only have the energy to answer one question or read one paragraph. That's perfectly okay. Give yourself permission to use this book however you like, whether it's reading one chapter at a time or jumping between questions as you go. There's no "right" way to approach it, just the way that works best for you.

So, let this book be a companion, a resource, and a friend along your journey. Whether you dive in for five minutes or five hours, know that every question you explore brings you closer to clarity. So take a deep breath, open to the page that speaks to you, and trust that even small steps forward are still steps in the right direction.

II

Ask Yourself these Questions Before Divorcing Your Partner

Chapter 1: Because Breakups Cost More Than Bad Netflix Shows

Divorce is no light financial decision. It's the kind of thing that sneaks up on you with hidden fees, like that surprise credit card bill after a "quick" online shopping spree. Sure, love is priceless, but divorce can come with a high price tag. Let's talk about why that matters, how to avoid emptying your wallet along with your heart, and why thinking through some key questions might actually save you more than just money—it could even save your sanity.

Let's start with the basics: Have you ever thought about what a divorce actually costs? I'm not just talking about lawyer fees and court costs, though they can be a huge part of it. There's also the price of new living arrangements, dividing up assets, maybe even child support or alimony. It's like signing up for a VIP subscription to one of life's least fun clubs. But the worst part? Many people dive into this process without really understanding just how financially draining it can be, and they end up with bills they never saw coming. So, the question to ask yourself right now is: *Am I ready to take on this financial marathon?*

But it's not just the direct costs that stack up. Have you thought about the emotional toll—and how that can lead to even more expenses? Therapy bills, nights out with friends to "forget about it," or maybe even retail therapy (that's the expensive kind of therapy where you shop like you're the lead in a rom-com trying to "find yourself"). And let's not forget that endless parade of binge-watching Netflix shows as a distraction. How many hours of scrolling through bad reality TV can you handle before you start feeling the pull to hit "next episode" just to avoid thinking about it? So here's the real question: *Is the financial fallout of divorce something I can bear, or am I just hoping it will magically work itself out?*

Now, I'm not here to downplay what you're feeling. Relationships are messy, complicated, and sometimes heartbreaking. But they're also investments, ones we pour time, love, energy, and money into for years. So before you make a life-changing choice, take a step back and ask yourself if you've exhausted all other options. Divorce isn't the only solution to unhappiness, and sometimes a few deep conversations (or maybe even a little couples therapy) could go a long way toward saving both your bank account and your mental health. So, let me ask you: *Have you tried to work things out, or are you tempted to take what seems like the simpler way out?*

Here's another angle to consider: What are you truly hoping to gain by ending your marriage? Are you after peace of mind, freedom, or just an escape from a tough situation? These are valid desires, but they're not always found in a lawyer's office. Sometimes, those same goals can be reached within the relationship you already have—maybe just with a few changes or a fresh approach. Divorce doesn't just change your relationship status; it changes everything, from your social circle to your financial future. So, ask yourself this: *What is it that I'm really looking for, and can I find it without tearing my life in two?*

And finally, there's one more question you should think about:

What if things could get better? What if the very things driving you crazy about your partner are things that could change with some effort, honesty, and the right support? Divorce can seem like a door leading to freedom, but sometimes it's just an exit you're sprinting toward because the path you're on feels too tough. So before you take that leap, think about the cost—not just to your wallet but to your heart, your future, and even your hopes for happiness.

Reflection Questions

1. What are my true reasons for considering divorce, and have I fully explored all possible solutions within my relationship?
2. How prepared am I to handle the financial consequences of a divorce, including hidden and long-term costs?
3. Am I looking for an escape or a chance to build a healthier, happier life, and is there another way to achieve that goal?
4. Have I thought about the emotional costs of divorce and what support systems I would need to cope with them?
5. If things could change for the better within my relationship, what specific changes would I need to see?

Practical Exercise

Create a "Cost of Divorce" worksheet. Write down every potential cost you can think of—from lawyer fees to therapy, new housing costs, even a monthly "emotional wellness" budget (for things like new hobbies or stress-relief activities). Look over the total, and ask yourself if it's something you're financially and emotionally ready to take on.

Action Plan

1. Schedule a quiet hour to reflect on the questions and fill out your "Cost of Divorce" worksheet.
2. Share your thoughts and reflections with a trusted friend or family member who can offer you a grounded, outside perspective.
3. Consider talking to a financial planner or therapist to get a clearer picture of the true costs of divorce.
4. Decide on one positive action you can take within your relationship today, whether that's a heartfelt conversation, a compromise, or even a date night to reconnect.
5. Revisit these questions and this action plan after a month to see if your feelings or situation have shifted.

Chapter 2: To Avoid Playing Ping-Pong with Your Feelings

Is it truly over, or is this just one of those "I-need-space" moments? Emotions in relationships can be as unpredictable as a reality show, with highs, lows, and cliffhangers. One day, you're convinced it's done; the next, you're reminiscing about the good old days. This back-and-forth can feel like a game of emotional ping-pong, and it's exhausting. If you're nodding along, let's talk about how to finally get some clarity on what you're really feeling and how to keep that paddle from swinging back and forth forever.

Let's start here: Have you noticed how our emotions can shift wildly depending on the situation? Maybe you're feeling disconnected after a rough week, and suddenly, every minor irritation seems like a sign that it's "the end." But then, one sweet gesture, one heartfelt conversation, and suddenly, you're rethinking the whole thing. Emotions are fickle, but here's the deal: they're not always the best guide for major decisions. Sometimes, those temporary waves of frustration or dissatisfaction are just that—temporary. So, the first question to ask yourself is: *Am I making decisions based on lasting truths or momentary feelings?*

Consider this: Relationships go through phases, just like the moon (except, maybe, with more drama). Some phases are light and easy, and others feel like dark, uncharted territory. It's normal to experience moments of doubt. But what if these doubts are just a normal part of being in a long-term relationship? What if the feeling of "I need space" is actually an invitation to look at what needs to change rather than calling it quits? So, before making any big decisions, ask yourself: *Is this truly the end, or am I just in a difficult phase that could eventually pass?*

Now, here's a question you might not have considered: *What's the real reason behind my feelings?* Often, the frustration or disconnection we feel is rooted in something much deeper than that annoying habit or recent argument. Maybe you're feeling unappreciated, bored, or like you've lost your spark together. Those are serious feelings, but they don't always mean it's over. Sometimes, they mean there's work to be done—by both of you. The difference between "I'm just frustrated" and "I'm ready to walk away" lies in figuring out what's really going on beneath the surface.

And while we're on the topic, let's be honest: the grass isn't always greener on the other side, but it can seem that way when you're feeling stuck. It's easy to think about what life *could* be like outside your relationship, imagining a world of peace and independence. But sometimes, it's less about the partner you have and more about the feelings you haven't fully explored. So before you start mentally redecorating a new life, ask yourself: *Have I fully processed what's happening in this relationship, or am I just fantasizing about an escape?*

The bottom line is, separating the "I-need-space" moments from the "It's-really-over" moments is a tough call. And it requires honesty—real honesty. Are you wanting space because you truly feel it's time to close this chapter, or are you craving some breathing room to get back in touch with yourself? Relationships aren't always easy, and the desire for space can be a healthy signal to pause and reflect rather than rushing to the exit. So ask yourself, with all honesty: *If I had more time, space, or support, would I feel differently?*

Reflection Questions

1. Am I feeling a genuine desire to end the relationship, or is this just a difficult moment that could pass with time?
2. What specific things in this relationship make me feel frustrated, and are these frustrations permanent or temporary?
3. Have I communicated my feelings to my partner, or am I expecting them to read between the lines?
4. Am I seeking a true ending, or am I craving change or growth within the relationship itself?
5. If my partner addressed my biggest frustrations, would I still feel the urge to leave?

Practical Exercise

Create a "What's Really Bothering Me" list. Write down the things that make you feel disconnected or frustrated in your relationship. Next to each one, label it as "fixable," "temporary," or "dealbreaker." This can help you separate the temporary frustrations from the deeper, unchangeable issues.

Action Plan

1. Set aside a quiet time this week to go through your "What's Really Bothering Me" list and look for patterns.
2. Talk to your partner about one or two things from the list that could be fixed or improved. See how they respond to your honesty.
3. Decide on one small, positive change you can make in your routine to help refresh your connection—something as simple as a "no phones at dinner" rule or a weekly check-in.
4. Make a commitment to revisit your list in a month to see if your feelings have shifted.
5. Reflect on whether your need for space or change has more to do with personal growth than ending the relationship. If it does, focus on actions that support growth within the relationship rather than seeking it outside.

Chapter 3: Because Grass Isn't Always Greener

Ah, the lure of the greener grass. When relationships get rocky, it's natural to look over the fence and wonder if life might be better on the other side. Maybe you're dreaming of freedom, picturing stress-free days, or imagining a fresh start. But here's the thing: that "freedom" can come with its own set of challenges, ones that aren't always obvious in the glow of imagined new beginnings. Before you jump the fence, let's dig into what you're really looking for and whether the grass is actually as green as it seems.

Let's start with a reality check: Have you ever wanted something so badly, only to find out that it wasn't quite what you'd imagined? Maybe you've idealized what life would be like post-divorce, picturing calm, order, and the freedom to do whatever you want. But real life is rarely as neat as it appears in daydreams. Often, the "freedom" you're craving also comes with loneliness, financial adjustments, and the challenge of navigating life solo. So ask yourself: *Am I envisioning an idealized future, or am I prepared for the reality that comes with it?*

And let's be real—single life has its ups and downs too. When you're feeling frustrated in your relationship, it's easy to imagine that life on your own would be simpler. No more compromise, no more constant consideration of someone else's feelings. But without someone there to lean on, the "freedom" you're picturing might also feel like isolation. Things that are easier to handle as a couple—financial burdens, home responsibilities, even simple companionship—suddenly become solo missions. So here's a question to chew on: *Am I ready to take on those responsibilities alone, or am I overlooking the positives of having a partner by my side?*

Let's talk about expectations for a moment. Many times, we imagine the life we *don't* have with rose-colored glasses, while seeing the life we *do* have with a magnifying glass on every flaw. That new life you're picturing may look sparkly from where you're standing, but what if those dreams are only shiny on the surface? Maybe the stress you're trying to escape would simply be replaced by a different kind. Maybe the feelings of frustration or boredom would follow you into any relationship—or any life situation—because they're signals from within you rather than purely from your partner. So ask yourself this: *Is it truly my relationship that needs changing, or is it my perspective on life?*

Then there's the issue of regret. Many people who go through divorce find themselves surprised by the "little things" they miss—small, everyday comforts that they took for granted. Maybe it's the morning coffee together, the unspoken understanding, or the shared routines that brought stability. Sometimes, it's these little moments that are hardest to live without, the ones that no amount of imagined freedom can replace. So here's a question to consider: *Are there small, meaningful parts of this relationship I would regret losing?*

Finally, before you leap to greener pastures, ask yourself one last thing: *Am I running from something, or am I running to something better?* It's easy to get caught up in the fantasy of "what could be" without fully acknowledging what might be lost. Ending a relationship should be about moving toward something positive and life-giving, not simply escaping what feels hard right now. So take a breath, ask yourself some honest questions, and make sure you're not seeing greener grass where there's really just a different patch of lawn.

Reflection Questions

1. When I think about life outside this relationship, am I focusing on idealized moments, or am I thinking through the realities I might face?
2. What specific challenges do I imagine my "freedom" will solve, and are these things I could also work on within my relationship?
3. Are there parts of this relationship—like daily routines, companionship, or shared memories—that I would miss or regret losing?
4. Is my vision of a new life truly about self-growth, or am I simply trying to escape feelings that may not change in a new relationship?
5. If I had to live with the decision I'm considering now, would I still feel it's the right one five years down the line?

Practical Exercise

Make a "Life Beyond the Fence" list. Write down all the things you imagine would be different if you were on your own—both the pros and cons. Try to be as realistic as possible. Think about things like finances, time management, daily routines, and emotional well-being. Review the list, and see if there are any things you might actually be able to achieve within your current relationship.

Action Plan

1. Block out 30 minutes this week to work on your "Life Beyond the Fence" list and reflect on it.
2. Share your thoughts with a trusted friend who can offer an outside perspective, helping you distinguish between daydreams and reality.
3. Pick one thing from your list that you can work toward within your relationship—whether it's more independence, a new hobby, or even some solo time.
4. Commit to a weekly reflection, asking yourself if your vision of "greener grass" is still the same or if it's evolving as you clarify what you truly need.
5. Check back in a month to reassess whether your need for freedom has shifted, and if so, consider what actions you can take to work on your personal growth *within* the life you have.

Chapter 4: So You Don't Have to Be Besties with Your Lawyer

Divorce can get real complicated, real fast. It's like stepping onto a legal merry-go-round, except there's no cotton candy or fun prizes, just a whole lot of paperwork and fees. Lawyers are great people, but let's be honest—no one wants to spend more time with them than necessary (or more money, for that matter). So before you dive into this complex, often costly process, let's dig deep to figure out what's *really* bothering you. Who knows? The solution might not require a single legal form.

Here's a good place to start: Have you pinpointed the core issues that are pushing you toward divorce, or are you ready to hand over the steering wheel to a lawyer and let them navigate your life? Divorce lawyers can help with legalities, but they can't solve the emotional or relational root causes of why you're considering a split. If you're not completely clear on what's driving this desire to separate, you might find yourself sitting in your lawyer's office, explaining issues that could've been addressed without getting the law involved. So ask yourself: *Am I truly ready for divorce, or do I just need clarity on what's not working?*

It's also worth considering how much of your frustration might come from miscommunication or unmet needs, rather than fundamental incompatibility. Often, we think, "It's over; we're just not on the same page," when in reality, we might be reading the same book but on different chapters. Have you tried spelling out your feelings and needs to your partner, or are you expecting them to pick up on subtle hints? Before pulling out the paperwork, make sure you've communicated openly. After all, lawyers are great at understanding legal jargon—not always emotional nuance. So the question is: *Have I done my part to communicate clearly, or am I assuming my partner already knows how I feel?*

And let's not forget about the practical side of things: Lawyers are expensive. A divorce can easily drain your savings, leaving you with less for the future you're envisioning. So if there's even a small chance you can solve the underlying issues without the cost of a lawyer, wouldn't that be worth a try? Think about all the things that money could go toward instead—therapy, a relaxing trip, even a fresh start within your relationship. Lawyers are great, but you probably don't want to spend your vacation fund on billable hours. So here's the question to ponder: *Could that money be better spent on improving my current situation rather than ending it?*

It's also important to think about the "after" phase—life post-divorce. The emotional, financial, and even logistical challenges don't end the day the divorce is finalized. There will still be hurdles to clear, like adjusting to new routines, potentially co-parenting, and managing divided finances. In many ways, the struggle continues long after the ink has dried. So ask yourself this: *Am I prepared for the challenges that come after divorce, or am I just focused on the challenges I'm facing now?*

Ultimately, getting real with yourself can save you from rushing into a process that's more stressful and complex than it might seem. Take this time to reflect on what's truly at the heart of your frustration, and consider if there's a different way forward. If the idea of spending months (or even years) hashing things out in a lawyer's office doesn't sound appealing, you're not alone. Sometimes, clarity, communication, and a little patience can make a huge difference without a single form filled out.

Reflection Questions

1. Have I identified the core issues in my relationship, or am I focusing on surface-level frustrations?
2. How thoroughly have I communicated my feelings and needs to my partner? Could there be any miscommunication that's amplifying our problems?
3. What would I prefer to invest in: repairing this relationship or ending it and facing the financial and emotional costs of divorce?
4. How much am I ready for the logistical and financial realities of life post-divorce, including changes to lifestyle, finances, and routines?
5. Would I feel relieved or regretful about spending time and money on a lawyer to solve my current issues?

Practical Exercise

Make a "Lawyer-Free Solutions" list. Write down every potential solution or step you could take to resolve your issues without involving legal help. Think about ways to improve communication, set boundaries, or resolve conflicts on your own. Review the list and see if there are any steps that feel realistic and helpful.

Action Plan

1. Take 15 minutes to create your "Lawyer-Free Solutions" list and prioritize the steps that seem most achievable.
2. Set aside time this week to talk with your partner about one or two items on your list and see how they respond.
3. Make a small financial plan for the future, considering how much money divorce might cost versus how you could use that money for personal or relationship growth.
4. Reassess your feelings in one month to see if these steps have helped ease your concerns or shifted your perspective.
5. If the issues still feel insurmountable, consider exploring mediation or counseling before committing to full legal action, giving yourself a chance to pursue a solution outside the lawyer's office.

Chapter 5: To Make Sure This Isn't Just a Temporary Road Bump

Every relationship hits rough patches. It's like driving down a bumpy road—uncomfortable, maybe even frustrating, but not necessarily a reason to ditch the car. Sometimes, though, those bumps can feel so constant and overwhelming that it's easy to think, "This is it; it's over." But what if what you're facing isn't a dead-end, just a rough patch that could smooth out over time? Let's explore how to tell if your relationship is going through a repairable dip or if it's truly time to turn back.

First, take a step back and think about other times you've felt frustrated or discouraged in your relationship. Has this feeling come and gone before? Relationships have their rhythms, just like seasons. Winter may feel cold and endless, but spring is always around the corner. The first question to ask yourself is: *Am I in a temporary winter phase, or has this feeling lasted so long that it seems more permanent than seasonal?* This can help you see if you're just in a down cycle that could eventually turn around or if this feeling is more persistent.

Now, let's think about the roots of the current rough patch. Is it tied to a specific event or situation, like a recent argument or a stressful life change? Sometimes what we think of as "relationship issues" are actually outside pressures spilling over into our personal lives. Maybe it's financial stress, family problems, or work pressure that's making everything feel harder. If that's the case, these might be temporary pressures that, once resolved, will bring some peace back to your relationship. So ask yourself this: *Are these feelings rooted in a specific event or challenge that could pass, or do they seem like permanent problems?*

Here's another angle: Do you still have moments of connection, fun, or intimacy with your partner, even in the middle of the rough patch? It's easy to focus on the negatives, but sometimes, the good moments are still there—they're just overshadowed by stress. Maybe you still laugh together or have moments of calm that remind you of why you're together. If those moments exist, they might be signs that there's still something worth holding onto. The question to reflect on here is: *Do we still have positive moments that show there's a foundation of love and connection, even if it's hard to see right now?*

Now, think about the long-term view: Are the things bothering you things that could realistically change? Not every problem can be fixed, but some things improve over time, especially when both partners are willing to work on them. Sometimes, our partners don't know what's bothering us until we clearly express it, and even then, it might take time to see changes. But if there's effort and potential for growth, that's a hopeful sign. So here's the question to ask yourself: *Are these issues things that my partner and I could realistically work through, or are they fundamental incompatibilities?*

And finally, there's the big question of regret. Imagine yourself a year from now, after having moved on from this relationship. Would you feel relief, or would you wonder if things could've gotten better with a little more time and effort? Sometimes, walking away is the best option, but it's important to be sure. Think about what you'll likely feel if you stay and work on it versus if you leave and close this chapter. So ask yourself: *If I were to leave right now, would I feel relieved, or would I look back and wonder if I gave up too soon?*

Reflection Questions

1. Have I felt this way before in my relationship, and did the feeling eventually pass?
2. Are my current frustrations tied to specific stressors that might be temporary, or do they feel like permanent issues?
3. Do I still feel moments of connection, fun, or intimacy with my partner, even in the midst of this rough patch?
4. Are the things bothering me things my partner and I could realistically work on and improve, or are they fundamental differences?
5. If I left now, would I feel confident in my choice, or would I worry I hadn't given my relationship enough time?

Practical Exercise

Create a "Rough Patch Tracker." Over the next two weeks, note down moments that feel frustrating and moments that feel positive in your relationship. Look for patterns—are the frustrations tied to specific situations or times of day? Are there positive moments that surprise you? This can help you see if the rough patch is as constant as it feels or if there's more ebb and flow than you realized.

Action Plan

1. Dedicate 10 minutes each night to updating your "Rough Patch Tracker" and observing patterns over two weeks.
2. Share one positive and one challenging observation from

your tracker with your partner and discuss how each of you can support each other through this period.

3. Identify one small action you can take daily to add positivity, whether it's a simple compliment, a shared moment, or just a few minutes of quality time.

4. Schedule a time for yourself in one month to look back at your tracker, reflecting on whether the rough patch has eased or persisted.

5. Revisit your reflection questions in a month and consider if you still feel the same or if your perspective on the relationship has shifted.

Chapter 6: Because Co-Parenting Isn't Exactly the Dream Team You Imagined

If kids are in the picture, divorce isn't just about you and your partner anymore—it's about the whole family. Parenting is a team sport on a good day, but co-parenting after a divorce? That's a whole new level of teamwork. While splitting up might seem like a way to find peace, it also means committing to an ongoing partnership with your ex for the sake of your children. Let's explore what co-parenting really looks like and ask the questions that help you figure out what's best for everyone, especially the little ones.

First, think about the kind of relationship you'll need to maintain with your partner post-divorce. Co-parenting requires communication, patience, and flexibility, which can be hard to come by when you're both dealing with the emotions of a breakup. Sure, the idea of "shared custody" sounds straightforward on paper, but the reality involves frequent coordination and discussions on everything from school schedules to bedtime routines. So here's a big question to consider: *Am I ready to keep this person in my life as a co-parent, even if we're no longer together?*

Now, let's talk about what this will mean for your children. Divorce is a life-changer for kids, and how you and your partner handle it will shape their experience and understanding of family. Stability and security are essential for children, and a peaceful co-parenting arrangement can go a long way in providing that. But achieving that requires both parents to stay committed to the same goal: prioritizing the kids' needs over their personal grievances. So ask yourself this: *Am I prepared to put my children's needs first, even if it means making compromises with my ex?*

Then there's the practical side of things. Co-parenting often means juggling schedules, creating routines, and sometimes even being flexible with holiday plans. If you and your partner don't see eye-to-eye now, think about how this might play out when you're trying to agree on school choices, activities, or rules for the kids. Co-parenting is a long-term commitment that requires you to work together even when it's inconvenient. So consider this: *Can I handle the practicalities of co-parenting, or am I envisioning a simpler process than what it might really be?*

It's also important to consider the impact this decision will have on your kids' emotional well-being. Divorce can be confusing and painful for children, who might not fully understand why their family is changing. As a co-parent, you'll need to be there to answer their questions, support their emotions, and help them feel safe. The strength of your co-parenting relationship can greatly affect their ability to adjust and cope. So ask yourself: *Am I ready to help my children through this transition, even if it means facing difficult conversations and emotions?*

And finally, think about the long-term picture. Co-parenting doesn't end once your kids turn 18. It continues through graduations, weddings, family holidays, and even grandkids. Are you prepared to share all these future milestones with your ex for the sake of your children? It's a lot to consider, but these shared experiences can either be a source of strength or tension, depending on how you approach them. So ask yourself this: *Am I ready to stay connected with my ex for the sake of my kids, not just now, but throughout their lives?*

Reflection Questions

1. Can I envision a healthy co-parenting relationship with my partner that benefits our children, even if we're no longer together?
2. Am I prepared to put my children's needs above my own feelings or grievances with my ex?
3. How flexible am I willing to be with schedules, routines, and plans to create a stable environment for my kids?
4. Am I ready to help my kids navigate the emotions of divorce and be there for their questions and concerns?
5. Can I see myself working with my ex as a team for important future milestones in our children's lives?

Practical Exercise

Create a "Co-Parenting Reality Check" list. Write down all the things you envision needing to coordinate with your partner if you were to separate—like weekly schedules, holiday plans, school activities, and discipline rules. Next to each item, rate how prepared you feel to handle each one in a co-parenting context. This can help you identify where your strengths and challenges lie.

Action Plan

1. Set aside 20 minutes to work through your "Co-Parenting Reality Check" list and honestly assess your comfort level with each item.

2. Have a conversation with a trusted friend or family member who has experience with co-parenting to get their insights and advice.
3. Identify one area from your list where you feel most challenged and brainstorm ideas for how you could manage it effectively if you were to co-parent.
4. Take time to discuss some of these realities with your partner if appropriate—especially if you're leaning toward separation. Honest conversations can help you both understand the practicalities involved.
5. In one month, revisit your list and reflect on any shifts in your perspective, keeping your children's needs at the forefront of your thoughts and decisions.

Chapter 7: To Unpack What's Really Wrong

Every relationship has its share of little annoyances—maybe it's the way they chew too loudly, leave socks on the floor, or have an odd obsession with rearranging the dishwasher. But if these small habits have started to feel like deal-breakers, it might be time to ask yourself: *Is this really about them, or is there something deeper going on?* Often, our irritation with these surface-level issues points to a larger, underlying disconnect. So let's dig in and see if we can uncover what's *really* bothering you.

To start, ask yourself how often these little annoyances seem to get under your skin. Are you finding yourself more irritated lately than usual? Sometimes, when we're dealing with deeper dissatisfaction, our tolerance for small things wears thin. What once felt like a quirky habit may now feel like the last straw simply because we're holding on to unresolved feelings or unmet needs. So, here's your first question: *Are these little habits suddenly unbearable because I'm feeling disconnected or frustrated in other areas of the relationship?*

Let's go a bit deeper. When you think about what bothers you, does it reflect a pattern of behavior rather than just a habit? For instance, if your partner is forgetful about plans, is it truly just about the forgotten date, or does it feel like they're not prioritizing your time together? Often, specific behaviors can trigger feelings of being overlooked, unappreciated, or even unloved. Take a moment to think about whether these small issues represent larger needs that aren't being met. Ask yourself: *Is there a deeper message behind what's bothering me, like a need for more attention, respect, or intimacy?*

Here's another angle: What do your arguments or frustrations typically revolve around? Are they about the same small issues, or do they eventually spiral into bigger, more emotional subjects? For many couples, small arguments become doorways into unresolved feelings—about money, intimacy, or even future goals. If your arguments tend to drift into bigger themes, it might be a sign that these issues are more than just surface-level annoyances. So ask yourself: *When I get frustrated, does it reveal a bigger issue that we haven't yet addressed as a couple?*

Consider your own needs and wants outside the relationship. Are you feeling fulfilled in your personal life, or are you expecting your partner to meet all of your emotional needs? Sometimes, what we think are relationship problems are actually personal challenges—like stress from work, unmet goals, or even lack of self-care. If you're feeling unfulfilled outside your relationship, it's easy to project that onto your partner, hoping they'll fill the gaps. So ask yourself this: *Am I relying on my partner to meet needs that I should also be fulfilling for myself?*

And finally, think about your relationship goals. Are you and your partner aligned on where you see things going? Misaligned goals can lead to feeling misunderstood or disconnected, which can easily manifest as frustration over small things. If your goals are different, even in subtle ways, it can create an underlying tension that seeps into everyday interactions. Ask yourself: *Are we working toward the same vision of our future, or is this disconnect reflecting a larger uncertainty about our goals?*

Reflection Questions

1. Are my frustrations over small things coming from a place of feeling disconnected or neglected in other areas of the relationship?
2. Do these surface-level irritations reflect deeper needs for attention, appreciation, or emotional support?
3. When we argue, do these disagreements often lead to bigger issues, hinting at unresolved topics we've avoided?
4. Am I expecting my partner to fulfill all my emotional needs, rather than addressing some of my own personal growth areas?
5. Are we aligned on our long-term goals, or is there a disconnect in what we envision for our future together?

Practical Exercise

Make a "Root of the Issue" list. Start by writing down the small things that have been bothering you. Next to each one, try to identify any deeper need or feeling it might represent—such as "forgetting our plans" representing a need for quality time, or "messy habits" reflecting a need for respect and consideration. This list can help you see if there are underlying issues that are worth exploring with your partner.

Action Plan

1. Set aside time this week to complete your "Root of the Issue" list and reflect on what each irritation may represent.
2. Share one of your deeper needs with your partner in a way that emphasizes how it can strengthen your relationship, rather than blaming them for any unmet expectations.

3. Identify one small action you can take to fulfill some of your own needs, like setting aside time for personal interests, stress relief, or even therapy, if helpful.
4. Revisit these questions in a month to see if your perspective has shifted or if the deeper needs you identified are being met more consistently.
5. Reflect on any patterns you've noticed in your frustrations, using them as guideposts for ongoing conversations with your partner about how to build a stronger, more fulfilling relationship together.

Chapter 8: Because Rebounds Aren't the Cure-All

The idea of a fresh start can be wildly appealing when things get rocky. A new beginning, a clean slate—it sounds like the perfect solution to all the stress, arguments, and unmet needs you've been struggling with. But here's the catch: sometimes, a "new beginning" is just the same old problems wrapped in a shiny new package. If you're thinking of ending your relationship for the possibility of finding something better, let's make sure it's the *right* choice, not just a quick fix.

First, let's consider what a new relationship actually brings to the table. Yes, there's the excitement of getting to know someone new, the thrill of fresh attraction, and the comfort of a blank slate. But before long, even the best new relationships settle into routines and bring their own unique set of challenges. The qualities that might bother you in your current relationship could very well crop up again, especially if they're linked to your own personal needs or patterns. So, ask yourself: *Am I truly ready to start fresh, or am I just looking for an escape from my current problems?*

Now, think about what's driving your desire for a new start. Is it a specific issue with your partner, or is it a general sense of discontent? Sometimes, we're so eager to "move on" that we overlook our own role in the relationship dynamic. If we don't take the time to unpack our own patterns, we may end up repeating the same issues in future relationships. A fresh start can be beautiful, but it's no substitute for personal growth and reflection. So, here's a question to consider: *Is my desire to leave my partner rooted in their behavior alone, or are there aspects of myself that I need to work on to build a healthy relationship?*

It's also worth thinking about what you'll be carrying with you if you move on. Breakups and divorces don't erase the history you shared or the emotional baggage that comes with it. They often bring new layers of complexity, such as hurt feelings, unresolved resentments, or regrets. And unless you're truly at peace with leaving, those emotions may follow you, casting a shadow on any new relationship. Before looking for a fresh start with someone else, ask yourself: *Am I emotionally ready to close this chapter, or am I just hoping that a new relationship will make me forget the past?*

Another angle to consider is whether the excitement of a new relationship could cloud your judgment. In the early days of any romance, it's easy to feel like every problem has melted away and that you've finally found "the one." But once the initial excitement fades, real life sets in, and you might find that the issues you faced before are still present, just in a different form. So ask yourself: *Am I seeking a new relationship for its true potential, or am I just hoping it'll fill the gaps my current one hasn't?*

Finally, think about what you'd miss if you walked away. When we're feeling trapped or frustrated, it's easy to focus on the negatives. But what about the shared memories, the inside jokes, the quiet understanding you've built with your partner over time? These things don't happen overnight and can be hard to replace. Maybe a fresh start sounds great, but it's worth asking if the life you have is worth fighting for—if there's still something left to build on. So ask yourself: *Am I focusing on the fantasy of a new beginning rather than appreciating the depth of what I already have?*

Reflection Questions

1. Is my desire for a fresh start based on a true need for change, or is it just an escape from my current challenges?
2. Am I willing to face my own patterns and needs, so I don't bring the same issues into a future relationship?
3. Have I truly let go of the emotional baggage from my current relationship, or am I hoping a new romance will help me forget the past?
4. Am I clear on whether I'm seeking a new relationship for genuine connection, or just as a "fix" for unmet needs in my current one?
5. What aspects of my relationship would I miss if I left, and have I fully considered whether they're worth holding onto?

Practical Exercise

Create a "New Beginning Wishlist" and a "What I'll Leave Behind" list. In the "New Beginning Wishlist," write down everything you hope a new relationship would bring you—such as better communication, shared interests, or more understanding. In the "What I'll Leave Behind" list, write the things you value in your current relationship that you may miss if you walked away. Comparing these lists can help clarify what you're hoping to gain versus what you'd be giving up.

Action Plan

1. Spend 15 minutes working on your "New Beginning Wish-list" and "What I'll Leave Behind" lists, reflecting on each item carefully.
2. Share one item from each list with a friend or trusted person for an outside perspective.
3. Choose one action you can take to address an item from your "Wishlist" within your current relationship—like having an open conversation about unmet needs or trying a new shared activity.
4. Check back on your lists in a month to see if your perspective has changed or if you feel a renewed connection with your partner.
5. Revisit your reflection questions in a month to consider whether the desire for a fresh start is still there, or if it's been replaced with a deeper appreciation for what you have.

Chapter 9: So You Don't End Up Wondering, "What If?"

Few feelings are as haunting as regret, especially when it comes to relationships. Ending a relationship is a huge decision, and the last thing you want is to walk away only to be plagued by endless "what if" questions. What if things could have worked out? What if I'd tried harder, communicated more, or just held on a little longer? The good news is that you can "regret-proof" your decision by looking at every angle, turning over each stone before you make a final choice. Let's dive into how to make sure you don't leave any questions unanswered.

First, think about the effort you've already put into this relationship. Have you truly done all you can to make it work, or have you been hoping for change without actively working toward it? Sometimes, we assume that if a relationship were "right," it would simply fall into place. But the reality is that even great relationships require intentional work. So ask yourself: *Have I done everything I reasonably can to improve this relationship, or am I leaving with unfinished business?*

Now, consider your communication with your partner. Often, "what if" regrets stem from not having fully shared our needs, boundaries, or feelings. Have you been completely honest about what you want and need? It can be easy to hold back, hoping that our partner will read between the lines or magically understand what's wrong. But real closure only comes when we've been open and honest. So here's the question: *Have I communicated my feelings as clearly as possible, or am I hoping my partner will just "get it"?*

Another angle to think about is timing. Relationships go through ups and downs, and sometimes, a low phase can make things feel worse than they really are. Are you considering ending things at a particularly tough time—like during a stressful work project, a family issue, or after a big argument? These things can cloud your perspective and make it harder to see the whole picture. If timing plays a role, it might be worth giving things a bit more time before making a decision. So, ask yourself: *Am I thinking about ending this relationship because of a temporary situation, or is this a consistent feeling that I've had for a while?*

Let's also talk about future possibilities. Think about what life would look like after this relationship ends. Does it feel like a positive, fulfilling move, or does it simply feel like an escape from a tough situation? It's easy to imagine a brighter future without the stress of the relationship, but consider the whole picture—how you'll handle the emotional, practical, and financial realities of a breakup. So ask yourself this: *Am I looking forward to a new chapter with excitement, or am I just trying to get away from my current one?*

Lastly, consider whether you'll miss your partner as a person. When relationships get tough, it's easy to lose sight of why you fell in love in the first place. But if you look back at the qualities that drew you together, would you still feel the same way? Are there things about your partner that, despite everything, you'll genuinely miss? If there's still love or connection there, it's worth thinking about whether that's something you're ready to let go of. Ask yourself: *Are there parts of this relationship that I'd regret leaving behind, or am I ready to close this chapter fully?*

Reflection Questions

1. Have I genuinely done everything I can to make this relationship work, or am I leaving with unfinished efforts?
2. Have I communicated my needs, feelings, and concerns as openly and honestly as possible?
3. Am I considering leaving during a temporary rough patch, or have I felt this way consistently over time?
4. Do I feel excited and hopeful about the future on my own, or am I mainly looking to escape my current situation?
5. Are there specific qualities in my partner that I'll miss, and am I prepared to let go of those things if I leave?

Practical Exercise

Create a "No Regrets" Journal. Write down each of the reflection questions above, and under each one, jot down your honest answers. Take your time with this, and let yourself be as open as possible. This journal can be a place to express any fears, hopes, or worries you have about ending or continuing the relationship. Reviewing it can help you make a decision that feels final and free of lingering "what if" thoughts.

Action Plan

1. Set aside a quiet hour to begin your "No Regrets" Journal, giving each reflection question thoughtful consideration.
2. If possible, share one key insight from your journal with your partner as a way to open up about any unresolved concerns or feelings.
3. Choose one action that represents your best effort to

49

improve the relationship, such as initiating an honest conversation, trying a new form of quality time, or seeking outside support.

4. Revisit your "No Regrets" Journal in a month to see if your feelings have changed or if you're closer to making a decision with full clarity.

5. Reflect on your answers to the questions and your recent efforts, asking yourself if you feel more at peace with your choice—whether that's to stay or to move on—knowing you've looked at every angle with care and honesty.

Chapter 10: Because Dating Apps are a Whole New Jungle

If you've been off the dating scene for a while, here's a heads-up: things have changed. Gone are the days of meeting people solely through friends or chance encounters. Now, it's all about swiping, messaging, and matching—a whole new jungle of dating apps, profiles, and algorithms. Dating apps are fast-paced, often confusing, and full of both possibilities and pitfalls. So, before you rush into divorce with dreams of finding someone new, let's take a realistic look at what modern dating is like and make sure you're truly ready for it.

Let's start with the basics: Have you thought about how dating has evolved? It's a world of profile pictures, witty bios, and swipe-right chemistry. It sounds easy enough, but the reality can be surprisingly challenging. You'll need to brush up on small talk, deal with ghosting (when someone vanishes without a word), and navigate countless profiles that often showcase people's best versions of themselves—sometimes at the expense of reality. So, before you dive in, ask yourself: *Am I ready to deal with the ups and downs of dating in today's app-driven world, or am I idealizing it as a quick path to happiness?*

Another thing to consider is the time and energy modern dating demands. It's easy to think you'll jump right back in, but dating apps can be a big investment of both time and emotional energy. Scrolling through profiles, engaging in multiple conversations, and coordinating dates can be fun, but it's also exhausting. And because dating is no guarantee of instant romance, you may end up facing a series of short-lived connections before finding anything meaningful. So here's a question to reflect on: *Am I prepared for the patience and resilience it takes to navigate dating apps, or am I hoping it'll be easier than my current relationship?*

Then there's the question of what you're truly looking for. Dating apps are designed to present a lot of options, but that doesn't necessarily mean quality matches are easy to find. If you're looking for a deep, meaningful connection, it might take more time than you think. It's easy to mistake the thrill of new connections for true compatibility, only to find that spark fading quickly. Before trading your current relationship for the thrill of something new, ask yourself: *Am I looking for genuine connection and long-term compatibility, or am I just craving something different?*

Let's also talk about the emotional side of modern dating. Going from a long-term relationship into the world of dating apps can feel like stepping into uncharted territory. You may experience excitement, frustration, and even loneliness as you navigate the highs and lows. The constant exposure to other people's seemingly perfect lives can sometimes amplify feelings of inadequacy or self-doubt, especially if you've been off the market for a while. Ask yourself: *Am I emotionally ready to put myself out there, or do I need more time to heal and strengthen my sense of self first?*

Finally, consider the impact this could have on your own expectations and standards. Dating apps can create a "grass is greener" effect, where the endless profiles make it tempting to keep searching for the "perfect" person. But perfection is rare, and real relationships require compromise and patience. Before you leave a relationship for the unknown, think about whether you're ready to navigate the jungle of modern dating or if there's still value in what you have. Ask yourself: *Am I open to the challenges of dating apps, or am I hoping for an idealized connection that may not exist?*

Reflection Questions

1. Am I ready to face the realities of modern dating, or am I idealizing it as an easy alternative to my current relationship?
2. Do I have the patience and emotional resilience to handle the ups and downs of dating apps?
3. Am I looking for a meaningful connection, or am I just craving something different from what I have now?
4. Am I emotionally prepared to enter the dating scene, or do I need more time to work on myself first?
5. Am I open to compromise and realistic expectations, or am I expecting to find a "perfect" person that may not exist?

Practical Exercise

Create a "Dating Reality Checklist." Write down the realities of dating that might challenge you, such as "investing time in conversations with strangers," "dealing with rejection," and "finding genuine connections." Next to each item, jot down how prepared you feel for that aspect. This checklist can help you see whether you're ready to start dating or if there's more you'd like to work on first.

Action Plan

1. Set aside 20 minutes to complete your "Dating Reality Checklist" and reflect on how prepared you feel for each aspect.
2. Talk to a friend who has recent experience with dating apps to get a better understanding of what to expect and gain an outside perspective.
3. Choose one aspect of dating from your checklist that feels particularly challenging and think about how you could prepare yourself for it, either emotionally or practically.
4. Revisit your checklist in a month to see if your readiness to date has changed or if you still feel more work is needed before you enter the dating scene.
5. Reflect on your answers to the questions and your checklist, asking yourself if you feel more clarity about whether dating apps are truly what you want or if staying and working on your current relationship is the better choice.

Chapter 11: To Spot the Difference Between Normal and Not-So-Not-So-Normal Conflicts

Every relationship has its share of disagreements, and arguments are often just part of the package. Some conflicts are simply part of the "welcome to marriage" starter kit, like bickering over whose turn it is to do the dishes or how to spend the weekend. But then there are conflicts that signal deeper issues—the ones that go beyond normal friction and may reveal red flags. Knowing the difference between the two is key to understanding whether you're dealing with typical relationship hurdles or something that might require a closer look.

First, think about how often these conflicts come up. Is it a once-in-a-while disagreement or a constant point of tension that just doesn't seem to go away? Minor frustrations that pop up occasionally, like arguing over who last left the lights on, are normal. But if you're rehashing the same issue again and again without resolution, it could point to a bigger underlying problem. So, the first question to ask yourself is: *Is this argument a rare occurrence, or has it become a pattern in our relationship?*

Now, consider the nature of the conflicts. Some disagreements are about day-to-day irritations—things like chores, personal habits, or how to load the dishwasher. These are common friction points in most relationships and can usually be worked through with a bit of compromise. But if the arguments are about core values—like respect, trust, or communication style— it's worth paying more attention. Core value conflicts often reveal fundamental differences that aren't as easily resolved. So ask yourself this: *Are our disagreements mostly about daily frustrations, or do they touch on deeper values that we might be fundamentally divided on?*

Another way to spot the difference is by examining how you and your partner handle conflict. Do disagreements end with resolution and understanding, or do they escalate and leave both of you feeling hurt or dismissed? In a healthy relationship, even disagreements should eventually lead to constructive dialogue or compromise. If your conflicts consistently leave you feeling resentful or misunderstood, it could be a sign that the dynamic needs work. So here's the question to consider: *Do our conflicts bring us closer to resolution, or do they create lasting resentment?*

Let's talk about respect. In any relationship, disagreements should still maintain a basic level of respect for each other's feelings and boundaries. Normal arguments might include raised voices or frustration, but they don't cross into personal attacks, name-calling, or belittling. If conflicts in your relationship cross that line, it's worth considering whether you're in a healthy space. Respect is the foundation of any relationship, and repeated disrespect in arguments is often a serious red flag. So ask yourself: *Do our arguments maintain respect, or do they frequently turn hurtful and disrespectful?*

Finally, think about how you feel after the argument. Normal conflicts may leave you feeling frustrated or drained temporarily, but there's usually a sense of relief or progress afterward.

However, if every argument leaves you questioning the relationship, feeling emotionally unsafe, or wondering if you're better off on your own, that's something to take seriously. Persistent feelings of doubt or insecurity after conflicts can indicate deeper compatibility issues. So, here's the last question: *Do I feel secure and understood after our arguments, or do I feel uncertain and doubtful about the relationship?*

Reflection Questions

1. Are our conflicts occasional and situational, or do they represent a pattern that keeps repeating?
2. Are we arguing about daily annoyances, or do these conflicts reflect deeper value differences?
3. Do our arguments lead to resolution, or do they create lasting resentment and unresolved feelings?
4. Do we maintain respect during disagreements, or do our arguments often cross into hurtful or disrespectful territory?
5. How do I feel after our arguments—relieved and understood, or insecure and doubtful about our relationship?

Practical Exercise

Create a "Conflict Log." For two weeks, make brief notes on any arguments you and your partner have. Record what the argument was about, how it was resolved (or if it wasn't), and how you felt afterward. At the end of the two weeks, review your log to see if there are any recurring themes or feelings. This log can help you identify if your conflicts are part of a pattern and whether they're more "normal" or "not-so-normal."

Action Plan

1. Set aside a few minutes after each conflict for two weeks to jot down your notes in your "Conflict Log."

2. Share an insight from your log with your partner, especially if it reveals something new about how you both approach conflict.

3. Choose one strategy to handle conflicts more constructively, such as taking a "cooling-off" break during arguments or focusing on using "I" statements to express your feelings.

4. Revisit your Conflict Log in a month to see if the nature of your disagreements has shifted or if certain issues are still recurring.

5. Reflect on your answers to the questions above and your Conflict Log to gain clarity on whether your relationship conflicts feel manageable and normal or if they're pointing to deeper issues that need addressing.

Chapter 12: Because You Deserve Clarity, Not Confusion

Divorce isn't an easy decision, and it often comes with a mix of emotions, doubts, and "what if" thoughts. But if there's one thing that can bring you peace of mind, it's clarity. Clarity is about knowing why you're making the choice, feeling confident in it, and not looking back with regret. So, before you take that leap, let's work through some questions that can help bring you that priceless clarity—so that, whatever you decide, you'll be standing on solid ground.

First, let's consider the reasons behind your decision. Are they coming from a place of self-reflection and growth, or are they rooted in temporary frustrations or external pressures? Sometimes, it's easy to confuse feelings of dissatisfaction with a desire for divorce, especially during stressful periods. Take a moment to ask yourself: *Am I making this decision based on a thoughtful assessment of my needs, or am I reacting to temporary emotions or outside influences?* This can help you ensure that your reasons are truly your own and not clouded by other factors.

Now, let's think about your vision for the future. Are you able to picture life after divorce clearly? What does it look like, and does it align with what you truly want? Visualizing your future can help you identify whether you're moving toward something positive or just hoping to escape something negative. Imagining life without your partner may clarify if this choice feels like a step forward or just a way out. So, here's the question to ponder: *Do I have a clear, positive vision of what my life would look like after divorce, or is my focus solely on leaving my current situation?*

Another crucial element of clarity is acceptance. Are you at peace with the idea of leaving, or does it leave you feeling anxious or regretful? Clarity comes when you're able to make peace with your choice—when you can look at the decision calmly and feel certain that it's the right move. If the thought of ending the relationship brings more relief than fear or sadness, it may be a sign that you're ready. But if it brings a sense of loss or uncertainty, it might indicate that you still have unresolved feelings. Ask yourself: *Am I at peace with the idea of moving on, or am I still wrestling with feelings of uncertainty or sadness?*

Let's also explore whether you feel you've given everything to this relationship. Clarity often comes from knowing you've left no stone unturned. Have you tried everything that's within your control to make things work, or are there actions you could still take to find resolution? It's much easier to find peace with a decision when you know you've put in every possible effort. So, the question here is: *Have I genuinely done all I can to make this relationship work, or are there steps I haven't taken that might bring me closer to clarity?*

Finally, consider what life might look like if you decided to stay and work on the relationship. Sometimes, clarity comes not from picturing an exit but from imagining what a renewed commitment might look like. If the thought of staying feels heavy or discouraging, it could be a sign that you're ready to move on. But if staying feels like it could bring growth or healing, it might be worth exploring that path further. So, ask yourself:

If I chose to stay and fully commit to this relationship, does that vision feel like a positive choice, or do I feel ready to let go and move on?

Reflection Questions

1. Are my reasons for considering divorce based on thoughtful reflection, or are they influenced by temporary feelings or external pressures?
2. Can I clearly envision a positive future for myself after divorce, or am I mainly focused on escaping my current situation?
3. Am I at peace with the idea of moving on, or do I still feel anxious, sad, or uncertain about leaving?
4. Have I truly done everything within my power to make this relationship work, or are there unresolved steps I could take?
5. If I chose to stay and fully commit, does that path feel promising, or does it feel like I'm forcing something that's no longer right?

Practical Exercise

Create a "Clarity Map." Divide a piece of paper into two sections. On one side, write down your reasons for leaving, and on the other, write reasons for staying. Next to each reason, add notes about how each one makes you feel—whether it brings peace, relief, sadness, or anxiety. Reviewing this map can help you find patterns in your thoughts and emotions, bringing you closer to clarity.

Action Plan

1. Take 20 minutes to work on your "Clarity Map," writing down your reasons for both staying and leaving, along with the emotions associated with each one.

2. Reflect on one item from your map that stands out, and spend a few minutes journaling about why it's so impactful for you.

3. Share a key takeaway from your Clarity Map with a trusted friend, counselor, or partner to get an outside perspective on your feelings.

4. Revisit your map in a month and see if your thoughts and emotions have shifted, helping you track any changes in your clarity.

5. Reflect on your answers to the questions above and your Clarity Map, aiming for a sense of peace and confidence in whatever decision feels best for you, knowing that you've thoughtfully considered every angle.

Chapter 13: What Now? You May Ask Yourself!

You've gone through the questions, explored the emotions, and examined every angle. You've done the hard work to find clarity, to understand your reasons, and to really see your relationship from all sides. Now, you might be left asking yourself, "What now?" It's a question that hangs in the air, carrying the weight of all those reflections, worries, and hopes for the future. You're standing at a crossroads, and while the path forward may still feel uncertain, you've already taken one of the most important steps—getting clear on what's truly best for you.

The first thing to remember is that it's okay if you're still not 100% certain. Very few life choices come with complete certainty. Choosing to stay or leave a relationship is no different. Instead of waiting for a lightning bolt of clarity, it can help to lean into the direction that feels most peaceful and right for you, even if it doesn't yet feel perfect. So, ask yourself: *Which choice brings me a sense of calm and confidence, even if it feels a little scary?*

If you're leaning toward staying, think about the steps you can take to make your relationship stronger and more fulfilling. What would need to change for you to feel happy, respected, and valued? Are there actions you and your partner can take together, such as improving communication, seeking counseling, or making time for shared goals? This can be an exciting opportunity to rediscover each other, work through those unresolved issues, and build a relationship that better serves both of you. So, consider this: *If I choose to stay, what concrete steps can I take to create the relationship I truly want?*

If you're leaning toward leaving, remember that this doesn't make you a failure. It simply means you're choosing to prioritize your well-being and future happiness. You've done the work to understand your needs, and now it's about stepping into that new chapter with confidence. You might feel nervous or even guilty at times, but remind yourself of the clarity you've gained. Ending a relationship can be painful, but it can also be an empowering decision when you're choosing it for the right reasons. Ask yourself: *What can I do to support myself emotionally and practically as I move forward into this new phase?*

Now, let's talk about what it looks like to move forward with intention, no matter which path you choose. Whether you stay or go, the reflections you've done here are powerful tools for growth. Carrying forward the insights you've gained about communication, self-care, and boundaries can shape your relationships in ways you may not have imagined. So, ask yourself: *How can I use what I've learned about myself and my needs to create a fulfilling future, regardless of my relationship status?*

Finally, remember that this decision, whichever way it goes, is part of your journey. Relationships, whether they last or not, teach us invaluable lessons about love, patience, and self-discovery. You don't have to have all the answers right now, and you're allowed to take each day as it comes. Life has a way of working out in ways we don't always anticipate, so trust in the journey, and know that clarity, peace, and fulfillment are all within reach.

Reflection Questions

1. Which choice feels the most peaceful and aligned with my future happiness, even if it's not 100% certain?
2. If I choose to stay, what specific actions or changes can help me create a stronger, more fulfilling relationship?
3. If I choose to leave, what steps can I take to support myself emotionally and practically during this transition?
4. How can I use what I've learned from this experience to improve my future relationships and personal growth?
5. What small steps can I take each day to honor my decision and move forward with confidence?

Practical Exercise

Create a "Path Forward Plan." Write down the choice you're leaning toward (staying or leaving) and list three specific actions you can take in the next month to support this decision. If you're staying, your actions might include working on communication, planning a date night, or scheduling counseling. If you're leaving, your actions might include seeking legal or financial advice, finding a support group, or creating a self-care routine.

Action Plan

1. Complete your "Path Forward Plan" and identify three specific steps to support your decision.
2. Share one action from your plan with a trusted friend or

counselor for encouragement and accountability.

3. Reflect on your feelings weekly to track your progress, observing any shifts in confidence, peace, or clarity.

4. Take one small step each week toward fulfilling your plan, allowing yourself grace and patience as you move forward.

5. Revisit your Reflection Questions and Path Forward Plan monthly to see if new insights or adjustments are needed, trusting in yourself to navigate this journey one step at a time.

Whatever path you choose, know that clarity is a gift, and you've given yourself a powerful foundation to build the future you deserve.

Conclusion: Embracing Your Choice with Confidence

Reaching a decision about your relationship is no small feat. You've walked through the emotions, dug deep into the questions, and faced some of the hardest truths head-on. Along the way, you've gained invaluable clarity about what you want, need, and deserve. Now, it's time to take all that insight and embrace your choice with confidence, knowing you've done the work to make the best decision for yourself and your future.

No matter which path you choose, remember that this journey has already transformed you. Every question you answered, every fear you faced, and every emotion you sorted through has shaped you into someone who's more self-aware, more resilient, and better equipped for whatever comes next. That's something to be proud of, regardless of the outcome. *You didn't rush the process. You took the time to honor your own needs, and that alone is a powerful step forward.*

If you've chosen to stay, then let this be a new beginning, an opportunity to rebuild with purpose and commitment. Let your relationship become a safe space for growth, communication, and respect. Remember the insights you've gained here and use them to create a relationship that truly aligns with your vision for happiness and partnership. Every relationship has its rough spots, but now you have the tools to navigate them with patience, understanding, and clarity. Embrace this renewed commitment and enjoy the possibilities it brings.

If you've chosen to move on, then take comfort in knowing that this choice, while difficult, is rooted in clarity and self-respect. Moving forward may feel bittersweet, but it's also an opening for a fresh chapter—one that's based on the lessons you've learned and the confidence you've built in yourself. Give yourself permission to grieve, heal, and grow, trusting that this decision is a step toward the future you deserve. Know that by choosing what's best for you, you're setting the stage for a life that honors your values, your needs, and your happiness.

And finally, whatever happens from here, remember to keep nurturing the relationship you have with yourself. At the heart of every question, reflection, and realization is a deeper connection to who you are. The clarity you've gained isn't just about this relationship—it's a foundation for every choice you make going forward. Honor it. Trust in it. And let it guide you, knowing that you are capable, worthy, and resilient enough to build a fulfilling life, whatever path you walk.

So here's to you—to the clarity you've earned, the courage you've shown, and the future you're creating. Life will continue to have its challenges, but you've proven that you can face them with honesty, thoughtfulness, and a steadfast commitment to your well-being. Take pride in this journey, and let it carry you confidently into whatever comes next. This decision, whatever it may be, is yours—and now, so is the future.

Wait...

WAIT...

I Need Your Help

If this book has helped you find a little more clarity, peace, or direction, I have one small request: would you mind leaving a review? Your thoughts and feedback don't just mean a lot to me personally—they can also make a big difference for others who might be searching for exactly this kind of support.

When you leave a review, you're helping this book reach others who are in the same boat, people who may feel lost, confused, or on the fence about a huge life decision. Your review could be the nudge they need to pick up this book, giving them a resource to find answers, insight, or even just a comforting reminder that they're not alone in their journey.

Think about the impact your honest review might have. Whether it's a few sentences or a detailed summary of what stood out to you, your perspective can offer real encouragement to someone else. It might be exactly what they need to feel seen, understood, and supported.

And if you're wondering what to say, there's no need for anything fancy or formal. Just share your experience—what you liked, what resonated, or how certain questions helped you see things more clearly. Even the simplest review can be meaningful to someone who stumbles upon this book at just the right time.

So, if you feel inspired, I'd be incredibly grateful if you could take a minute to leave a review. Together, we can help more people find the support they need, one honest review at a time. Thank you for being part of this journey—not only for yourself but for others who may benefit as well.

www.ingramcontent.com/pod-product-compliance
Lightning Source LLC
Chambersburg PA
CBHW052338220526
45472CB00001B/474